The Weight I Carry
By Aaron Fields

Copyright © 2025 Aaron Fields. All rights reserved.

Published by The Write Perspective, LLC

All rights reserved. No part of this book shall be reproduced or transmitted in any form or by any means, electronic, mechanical, magnetic, photographic including photocopying, recording or by any information storage and retrieval system, without prior written permission of the publisher. No copyright liability is assumed with respect to the use of the information contained in this book. Even though every precaution has been taken in preparation for this book, the publisher/author assumes no responsibility for errors or omissions. Neither is any liability assumed for any damage that results from the use of the information in this book.

ISBN: **978-1-953962-70-6**

🧠 DEVELOPMENTAL GOAL:

It's imperative that we help children understand that their world is made up of different layers—family, school, neighborhood, media, culture—and that all these things work together to shape how they feel, learn, and grow.

"Hello,

I hope all is well. I'm just a young boy but sometimes, the world forgets. They see danger in my joy. They hear trouble in my voice. They either don't care or forget I'm still learning how to be me."

"The people I see every day-------

They're supposed to protect me, love me and teach me.

But sometimes they look past me.

Or only look when I mess up."

"When no one listens, I stop talking.

When no one asks how I feel, I carry it all myself.

But I'm still little. I need someone to notice."

"Mama comes to school, but they talk over her.

They use big words to say I'm a problem.

But nobody talks about how I feel,

Or what I'm good at."

"When my school and my home don't talk together,

They miss who I really am.

I get caught in the middle."

"Papa works two jobs.

He's always tired.

He can't come to my games.

I wish he was around more."

"The people who make the rules don't live where I live.

But their choices still change my life. I wish my own community would do something about it."

"On the news, boys like me are 'dangerous.'

In books, we're barely there.

In stores, people stare."

"These stories shape how people treat me.

Sometimes I wonder if I can ever be enough.

But I didn't ask for these stories.

Maybe I should create my own narrative."

"At 5, they said I was 'too active.'

At 8, they said 'too loud.'

At 10, they say I'm 'a problem.'

What will they say when I'm 15?

Preschool

2nd Grade

5th Grade

"Each year, the weight gets heavier.

Not because I'm changing,

But because they stopped seeing me as a child."

"I carry the silence,

The stares,

The stories,

The rules made without me"

"I carry it all…..

But I shouldn't have to. At least not now"

"I don't need more labels.

I need someone to see me.

To speak up for me.

To teach me how to carry the world without letting it crush me."

"I'm still growing.

It's hard to grow right when the world around me doesn't change for the better.

I must learn how to change for myself regardless.

"I'm not broken.

I'm not a problem.

I'm a brilliant, beautiful boy who deserves to grow the right way."

Ecological System & Developmental Impact

Microsystem

Developmental Impact: Lack of attunement, under nurturing, over-surveillance leads to low self-esteem, anxiety, and acting out as a form of unmet needs

Mesosystem

Developmental Impact: Disconnection between home and school leads to mistrust, lack of coordinated support and miscommunication.

Exosystem

Developmental Impact: Unseen institutions (job, housing school boards) shape opportunity and stability. When those systems are inequitable, and the community becomes dysfunctional, Black children suffer silently.

Macrosystem

Developmental Impact: Stereotypes, underrepresentation, and media bias shape self-perception and lead to internalized oppression or resistance.

Chronosystem

Developmental Impact: Adultification, persistent labeling, and lack of support compounds developmental trauma, leading to negative mental health outcomes, disengagement from school, and difficulty in forming secure identity.